I, UNICORN

Use Quarantine

To Get

Enlightened Now

Natasha Ewendt

Cover design: V K Tritschler & M R Gudzenovs
Created at canva.com. Image from openclipart.org

CONTENTS

FOREWORD

By Daniel Mitel, internationally renowned
meditation master & School of the Heart leader

Want to find peace? Understand life? Meet the divine and get enlightened fast—without religion or philosophy? Then you've landed in the right place.

For those of you who are struggling in isolation or need a boost of energy and positive thoughts, for all who enjoy a dose of humor with your spirituality, this is the book you've been waiting for. Natasha has combined the best humor with powerful exercises that can bring a huge difference to your life.

Ever wished you could meet your higher self, or divinity itself? Natasha will show you how, and you won't believe how easy it is. Packed with aha moments, this revolutionary quick-read answers the cry for a simple guide to finding peace, for seekers of all ages. It explains divinity and enlightenment, mindfulness and meditation, in a conversational style anyone can understand, with plenty of laughs along the way.

Don't take life so seriously. Exactly! Remember that all around us is a dream and we are the powerful creators of this dream. And sometimes we need to stop. Stop everything we do; stop everything we think. And trust that every experience is a mentor, a master, a teacher! Let this heaven-sent guide show you the way.

GET UNICORNED

So you just used the last square of unicorn toilet paper. You've *Halo*'d and binged *Lucifer* till your ass is flat. And all that honky bonk has done its bit for the Christmas baby boom. What now?

Good question. The answer is that: Now.

There's never been a better time to learn to live in the now than er, now. And doing so is even more fulfilling than the final season of *Breaking Bad*. Pinkie swear.

If you feel like you sorta could be using your quarantine better, or if self-isolation is taking your basket casery next level, here is where you'll find insta-peace. If restrictions are easing where you are but you're worried about future waves, struggling to adjust to the New Normal, or feel the trauma will stay with you for awhile, these few pages will show you how to get anxiety to GTFO. If this book is landing on you post-apocalypse, it all still applies. This timeless guide is a fast, easy toolkit for managing anxiety, mastering yourself, and becoming enlightened. Actually.

You might think you're not fussed about reaching enlightenment, probably because the concept is so misty it's hard to understand. Many think enlightenment is a thing for nuns and monks and hardcore devotees, and to get it you need to meditate under a perpetual shower of unicorn pee while balancing on one toe that's being slowly eaten by dung beetles. But it's easier than you think, and deep down, we all want to be enlightened. We all want to unite with the divine.

WTF is enlightenment? This practical guide will tell all. Who am I to spout about enlightenment? I'm no nun or devotee, just a meditator. Ergo, if I can reach enlightenment, so can you. All I had to do to get enlightened was meditate regularly for a few months while on extended leave from my journalism gig. It was through enlightenment that I learned mindfulness, detachment and so on. But because my earlier spiritual experiences laid the foundation for enlightenment, I'll show you ways to shortcut the process and supercharge your evolution.

Before we tuck into those, lemme explain.

DUNG BEETLEMANIA

Enlightenment, or satori, is meeting yourself. It's a moment of revelation that unmasks your earthly self and reveals your divine self.

Spirituality paints the enlightened soul as a puddle of bliss and giggles riding a rainbow made of angels. Is there truly any such unicorn? Yes, yes there is. And you can be that unicorn. You already are that unicorn. You're already enlightened, but your naturally enlightened state is clouded by programming. By peeling back the program you can find your true self again—you can find everything you've been searching for.

Your program is a fun-bundle of neuroses and snarkery that traps you in delusion, or what I call the sim. You've probably heard some version of simulation theory, that our reality is essentially a generated program. The evidence is in front of you. Any object you look at is kinda not there. It's 99.99% empty quantum particles that only exist when they're being observed. Reality's no sure thing. True reality lies beyond those there/not there particles. It's the thing that generates them.

Here's where we get to the part about the divine. Don't bolt on me—it's not what you think. The Great Spirit, Goddess, God, the Source, the Force—call it Milo or Myrtle if it tickles your pickle—whatever you name it, it's all the same thing, and it's not how it's portrayed. It isn't an angry Gandalf in the sky. It's not a dictator, or even a person. If you have to label it at all, it's a united consciousness. And you're part of it. You are it. Under the meat suit, you're a chunk of infinite awesome. All that awesome awaits your discovery.

Mindfulness is the first step. It anchors you in the now, where you're not stressing about the past or future but focusing on the flow of the moment, which is your natural divine state. Meditation is phase two, going deeper into the now, into yourself. Then comes enlightenment, an amazing experience where you finally touch your true nature and suddenly everything makes sense.

Enlightenment is not exclusive to monastics. We tie it to them because they live in seclusion with few worldly distractions, making it easier for the veil between the sim and the true reality to fall. Right now we're all nuns and monks, metaphorically. Through quarantine, the divine is handing us enlightenment on a platter.

So now you know you don't have to get wimpled or dung beetled to get enlightened. Before we hack the how, we'll laser in on the why.

MEAT SUITS R US

Mindfulness, meditation and enlightenment raise your vibration, your personal frequency. The higher your vibe, the more divine access you get, and the more amazeballs things you're capable of. Enlightenment opens the door to mastery, where you'll find miracles, telepathy, telekinesis, and other such awesomeness. Basically, it's the door to god consciousness, Christ consciousness, Buddha nature, whatever you label it. It's becoming that rare creature, that blissy puddle of giggles. To get enlightened is to get unicorned.

Advanced enlightened masters use divine energy to conjure, levitate, bilocate, dematerialize and so forth with techniques like Kriya Yoga, which requires initiation and can't be taught in books. Levitation and sorts can also happen spontaneously without these methods, like it did for St Teresa. Once you're super advanced you can ascend—raise your vibe to permanently leave the earth plane for a higher one. You then take up a new residence on an astral planet or in a celestial or godly realm as a god, angel or other higher being.

However, learning tricks isn't the point of self-mastery. The point is union with your divine self, for the sake of your sanity and humankind.

Becoming a unicorn is one of the greatest contributions you can make to the world. The more of us become enlightened, the more enlightened society becomes, and the better life is for everyone, especially because we're all one. All that infinite awesome under your meat suit is not only limitless light, it's connected. Strip the suits and we're all one light. You can see this if you sit quietly with your eyes unfocused. After a while, you'll see a white halo around whatever you're looking at. The object might even disappear and become white light. That's divine light, people.

SURRENDER AND WIN

Before you can conjure a never-ending bag of Doritos from the astral realm or ascend into a world made of crystal, you need to master your thoughts and feelings so they no longer master you.

Self-mastery should start with surrender. Just get a surge of defiance? The word surrender will do that. All pumped up on our free will, none of us likes the idea of surrendering to anything. Thing is, till you surrender to the divine, you're blotting it out.

Consider it less like surrendering and more like uniting. You are divinity. You come from the source, and you're still part of that source, pretending for now to be human. Surrender to that source and you surrender to yourself, your higher self. The one who actually knows what this whole rodeo is about. The one who knows exactly where you need to go to find happiness. You're not surrendering at all, but uniting with your own divinity. So view it as a union. By yielding to the divine—you—you're coming home.

Surrender demands trust, which isn't easy unless you've experienced paranormal phenomena. Build faith by Googling real life stories about miracles, the supernatural, the beyond, whatever you need to know is real. This will open your consciousness to miracles so you can experience them yourself; then, seeing is believing. *Autobiography of Yogi* by Yogananda, which you can read free online, helped me.

The sooner you surrender, the sooner you end the struggle of earthly incarnations and move to higher realms. Whatcha waiting for?

To start your divine union, try saying this sacred Sanskrit mantra verbally or mentally every night before sleep or as you go about your daily business: *Om namo narayani.* This means *I surrender to the divine.* Before you go all frizzly, remember that by *surrender to* I mean *unite with*. If you say this mantra on loop with total faith, the sacred may open up to you in dazzling ways. I only had to do it for a short time before divinity first appeared to me.

Comfy with the idea of surrender—I mean union? Spiffy. Now we can mosey along to self-mastery.

CALM YOUR COCKLES

Your mind is a great tool for navigating the sim, but in the frenetic modern world, it's overworked. It's begging for a chance to chill, and it needs it if it's going to hook you back up to the divine. But your brain's been programmed for stress, so if you want serenity, you gotta reprogram. The quickest way to retrain your brain and master yourself is with one word:

Be.

That's it. Stop doing and thinking and be. Just being is how you feel the divine, because that's your natural state right there. That stillness when you manage to center yourself, that teeny bundle of calm in your cockles, is your divine essence. You can make it bigger and louder by taking more time to be. In time, this will get you unicorned.

To be or not to be is the pickle. Some find it hard to be still. The key is another single word:

Breathe.

A deep breath disengages the fight or flight center in your brain, switching the stream to the sacred. Instantly you feel your heart rate go down, your thoughts slow, your muscles unbunch. Take more deep breaths and calm will come.

Master yourself with your breath, and you can start to detach from the thoughts and feelings that keep you frazzled.

BE YOUR OWN BOSS

You've soothed yourself with some slow, steady breaths. Now it's time to quit letting your brain be your boss. May the reprogramming begin.

Rewiring your brain isn't a matter or fighting your thoughts. Anything you fight will fight back. Rather, accept and embrace everything. Whatever's happening, it's all part of the divine plan. Accept that your head's a minefield or your thoughts are squirly. Stop trying to squish them; it'll only make them worse. Embrace your active mind and thank it for trying to keep you safe. Then, help it out by detaching from your thoughts.

Take an objective look at the first thought that bobs up. Then realize it isn't *real*. That thought is just a teeny spark of energy in your gray matter, running along a well-worn neural path created years ago by someone else who programmed you. It isn't the definitive truth; it's only an idea. To glom onto it and react to it gives it a crapload of power it doesn't have. How big is a neuron? Smaller than the dot on this i. That's the thing you're handing all your power to.

Anxious thoughts seem to have tons of power. But

how often does what you fear happen? That's a whole lot of time, energy and brain-shrinking cortisol wasted on FA. Sure, it's good to be prepared. But when preparation goes beyond logic and due caution and into fear, not so great. Fear is a strong energy that lowers your vibration and blocks out divine vibes.

Disconnecting from fear robs its power so it no longer robs yours. Fear, like all your other bits, has a function. It's your survival instinct's alarm, but your program can nudge it out of balance. And a collective trauma like the one we're experiencing can trip your alarm even when you know you're doing the right thing to be safe. When anxiety persists against logic, keep grounding yourself in the moment, pointing out to your fear: see? In this moment we're okay, so quit worrying. If challenges come, you can find the tools to tackle them. Take back your power by thanking your fear and telling it there's no immediate danger. If it won't STFU, mute it.

This is easier when you take the next step: observing thoughts without judging or engaging with them. Don't react. See the thought merely as data and if it's irrelevant, delete. The apocalypse has taught us which services are essential and non-essential; assess thoughts in the same way. Letting go of non-essential thoughts—brain spam—frees up space for productive ones.

See which aspect of your program your thought has arisen from: antagonistic programming, people pleasing, anxiety, defiance. In time, recognizing where your thoughts come from means you can call 'em out and quit them before they truly begin.

To take this further, each time spam hits your inbox, focus instead on your breath. Be one with your breath (divinity) as often as you can, and spam—and pretty much everything—will bother you less. Unicornism comes closer this way.

TAME THE SAD PANDA

Detaching from feelings can stop an overreaction based on your program from turning a non-issue into a *Real Housewives of New Jersey* smackdown. But while it's good not to let emotions take over and make us do stupid, it's also vital to face our feelings and use them.

Emotions are trying to tell you something, usually that something is wrong and needs fixing. But many of us shut them down because we don't have the emotional tools to deal with them, or we do it to keep the peace, or to trade off for what we want. Or we don't suppress our feelings at all and wallow in them instead of doing something about them. Worse, we react instinctively and lash out, mangling our relationships.

As a feeling arises, examine where it's come from. Taking a moment to put it under a microscope means you're not so much at its mercy. Randomly pissy? Backtrack to find the cause. Often anger comes from fear or an offense to pride. Feeling like a sad panda for no reason? There's always a reason. You might've buried grief over a loss or bad experience and it won't go away until you front up to it. Or you might be feeling trapped or blocked and not sure how to get out. Meditate on it. I'll cover medo soon.

Whatever you're feeling, name it, face it, and either take action or if you can't, let it go. Apologize, forgive, make amends, make a change, whatever it takes to turn discontent into content. Forgiveness and amends have epic power that can bust your energy open to the miraculous. Catch is, you gotta mean it. Do the inner work till you do.

Where you can't take action and you have to let go, try writing out your feelings on paper and rip it up or burn it. Alternatively, Google the empty chair exercise or other ways to ditch your demons. The past will only poop on your present and future till you face it.

Self-forgiveness is paramount. It's true that you can't love anyone until you love yourself. Quit judging your blunders. We're all here to screw up, specifically. That's how you evolve, by messing up and learning from it. Expecting perfection from yourself is ludicrous. As a divine spark you're already perfect. You just have to break the spell of the sim to uncover that spark.

Rather than judge yourself for your booboos, look for the lesson. What did your mistake teach you about yourself? Guilt is a waste of life. We make mistakes so we change and evolve to the next level. That's all. Quit facepalming, look at the good things you've done, and award yourself awesome points. Until you come to peace with yourself, you can't come to peace with life. Denying your flaws won't erase them, and they have virtues, in the same way that your virtues have flaws.

Merits and faults are two-sided coins. Stubbornness equals determination. Compassion equals subjugation. Being aware of both sides of yourself means you can bring them into balance—be compassionate without subjugating yourself, strategic but not pathological, kind without sacrificing self-respect. Then you can use both your flaws and virtues for good. Stow the whip and start being proactive. Look at yourself honestly—both your flaws and your virtues—and make a list of how you can use both to improve yourself, your life, and the world.

GET GRRR

So you're mastering your thoughts and feelings with observation, acceptance and letting go. The next thing to apply this to is your animal nature.

We're human animals. For some, this is uncomfortable. We like to think we're all about the logic and self-control, but, well, we're not. Instinct accounts for much of our behavior, but because we're so set on not viewing ourselves as animals, we're mysteries to ourselves. And so life drags us along blindly.

Millennia of civilization has not made us entirely civilized. The popularity of gory-glory entertainment— our own in-home Colosseum—tells us our inner animals are very much alive and done being caged.

Your inner animal is nothing to fear. Like anything,

accept and embrace it. Once you stop fighting it, you can use it. Your animal has as much value as any other part of you, but when you don't understand it, you fear and squash it. This makes it angry ... and you won't like it when it's angry. Oppress your animal, it Hulks out. Nobody puts Hulky in a corner.

Everything exists for a reason. Your animal gives you strength and self-worth. To deny it is to deny those qualities, but you need them if you want to become a god. They're the upside. The downside is that most instincts are about protecting the self, and being unaware of them means you act selfishly and cause oodles of harm to yourself and loved ones.

Evolution is the shift from animal to god. If you want to do all that unicorny stuff—master yourself, see other realities, levitate, ascend into godly realms—you need to unplug from the sim's survivalist fear and plug into divine trust. That's hard until you've experienced the sublime and felt its miracles. You'll get a taste once you shut out the sim—your stressful programming, society's fear-mongering—and go within, to where divinity's hanging out, waiting for you to join the hootenanny.

See the animal instincts in yourself and their biological function. This crisis has put a spotlight on our survival instincts. Witness, the TP shemozzle. It's animal nature to hoard in loco times.

You can't kill instinct, but you can recognize where your instinctive reactions are doing harm and control them, for everyone's benefit. The more we act for the good of one and all, the better we survive.

It's also instinct to avoid suffering, but our hardships are what make us great. Every challenge makes you stronger, smarter, better. So don't run from your pain. Embrace it, use it, look for the lesson.

Accepting and understanding instincts takes the edge off and lends you self-compassion, which is primary on the path to unicornism. Explore your inner animal in meditation and make peace with it so you can use it for good.

The point of detaching from thoughts, feelings and instincts isn't to go Robocop, but to shuck the delusion of the sim so divine perception can get in. Self-awareness also stops you overthinking and complicating so that you can KISS—Keep it Simple, Squirtle. The simpler you make your life, the more room there is for divinity.

THE NOW IS WOW

Ahh. Here we are, all at peace with our thoughts and feelings and psycho little monsters. Now we can really get our teeth into mindfulness.

Like I said, mindfulness is staying in the now, not letting your awareness toddle into the past or the future. To do that effectively, first take the steps I outlined about purging your past so it stops yanking you back, and chilling your thoughts and feelings so you can rationally plan the future where necessary without freaking out about it. Then you'll find it easier to stay in the now.

Mindfulness is simple. When the fear gremlin creeps in and makes you panic about things you can't control, let it go and focus on what you're doing in that moment. When the guilt gremlin creeps in to remind you of your screwups, let it go, and focus on what you're doing in that moment. Take action and make notes for things to do only if it's important. Otherwise, don't engage with thoughts you know are non-essential.

Being mindful also gives you pause to think before you speak or act, swerving all kinds of curly. This self-awareness and accountability helps you see your true motives and call BS on yourself and others. It also cuts negativity. Low-vibe negative energy shields out positive energy, so use mindfulness to discard negative thoughts as they land.

As well as helping you detach from thoughts and feelings, mindfulness helps you detach from people and events. That's not to say you shouldn't care about anything. But the more you buy into drama, or depend on something or someone to make you happy (when actually you're God, which *is* happiness, so if you tap into that there's nothing else you need), the more people and events control you. They keep you locked in the sim and blocked from the sacred.

HAND IT OVER

Detachment becomes easier when mindfulness and meditation bring you into contact with the sublime.

Touching that grace and joy gives you first-hand experience that a force greater than you has planned your life and is guiding you, so you don't have to buy into the sim. Whatever concerns arise, hand them over to the divine and forget about them, trusting divinity to bring a solution.

Try doing this even if you're not a believer. Give your problems to the divine. Take positive action and seek solutions—teamwork is necessary. But once you've done what you can, let it go, knowing it'll be taken care of.

NAVEL LINT: DON'T EAT IT

There are no rules to reaching enlightenment. In the right headspace, it could happen spontaneously while you're picking bellybutton fluff. But meditation gives you a leg up by raising your vibration.

Your body contains a crapton of divine portals. Chakras are the main guys. There are also lotsa tiny meridians feeding in divine energy. The higher your vibration, the more energy gets through, and the stronger your connection with divinity and higher spheres. But tension and thoughts create static that drowns out divine energy. That's why medo is useful.

"I can't meditate! My mind is too busy!" You're not the only one. That's the challenge for all of us—stilling the mind enough for divinity to get a say. It's not mission: impossible. All you need to do is deep breathe, be in the now, and watch your thoughts. If you think you can't possibly meditate, think of a time when you finally mastered a skill you never thought you could. You can do it again.

Come meet the place in your brain called *Ahhhhh*. Medo brings zen, health and happiness. It can even make your brain bigger. What's not to like? Healing, facetiming higher beings, hacking yourself—it's all rad.

FIND YOUR HAPPY CORNER

I've simplified this medo method at the end of the book, but here it is in more detail so you can soak it up.

First, make sure you're lying or sitting comfortably with your spine relatively straight (don't force it if it hurts). You can medo with your eyes either closed or focused slightly down at a 45 degree gaze.

Then picture yourself wrapped in a protective bubble of divine white light. Do this before any spiritual practice. It's like locking the door on any undesirables that might wanna say howdy. You can also do it before sleep for sweeter dreams and before you go out. If any unwanted spirits manage to poke through, call on whatever higher being you believe in to cart them off.

Recall how you're one with divinity? Use this to your advantage. To get into medo and keep bringing your mind back when it scutters off, focus on your breath. You can count your breaths, or focus on the feeling of your chest rising and falling. Better yet, focus on the connection between your breath and the divine with this trick divinity taught me. Your breath is divinity's breath, the life that sustains you. So when you inhale, imagine the divine is saying, "You." When you exhale, imagine the divine saying, "Me." You ... and me. You ... and me.

Next, let your body soften. Relent every dollop of tension, starting with your facial muscles, shoulders and back, to that knot in your stomach, to your toes.

Now, because you're finally still, thoughts will go bananaballs for your attention. Remember, observe them rather than judging or engaging with them. Don't be so *in* them. Or give them a positive focus in the form of a mantra, repeated aloud or in your head. Use a mantra to get into meditation; once you're in, stop, and enjoy. *Om namo narayani* is great for this. You can also use a manifestation mantra, eg "I command you Goddess/God/Myrtle to bring me enlightenment now." Divinity digs being commanded, because it loves to see you recognize and use your divine power. Don't expect your wish to manifest instantly, but if you have faith and trust, don't be surprised if it happens fast.

If you're way too active to be still, try Hatha yoga, walking meditation, integrated mindfulness, Nike's running meditation app, tantric sex, anything that gets you closer to the divine.

Once you've stopped the hamster wheel in your head, simply soak in the quiet, or self-hack. Take this rest to navel-gaze and find yourself. Then use it to elevate. To get enlightened faster, combine this medo with the medos at the end of the book.

Meditating each day, preferably first thing before your program kicks in and takes you on a brain spam rampage, is the ideal. If you can't manage that, aim for a few times a week or once a week. More medo means faster enlightenment.

Meditate for five minutes at first, then ten, then stretch it out. The more you medo, the longer you'll be able to, and the deeper you'll go. In time you'll start connecting with something beyond the sim. It may begin with inner energy waves, divine sounds like bells or rain, or mental images that are murky like alphabet soup, clarifying as your third eye opens. There may come physical changes like heart rate elevation or feelings of pressure, sinking or falling. This is your physical vibe climbing. Ride it out and you'll find yourself in altered consciousness, the astral realm, maybe even the divine plane. It helps if you trust in your guides.

YODEL FOR YODA

Your spirit guide is your Yoda, your golden ticket to the other side. We all have guides, usually a few, along with guardian angels, corny as it sounds. Call on them to guide you. Know that they're with you and whatever happens in medo is them taking you by the hand and showing you the way in their language. You might sense, hear or see them, or be given a name or shown a symbol to connect the pair of you. Whatever happens, run with it.

KNOW YOUR RADNESS

Okay. You've crushed surrender (*union*, I mean union), mindfulness and meditation. The final key is self-care.

Needless to say, fitness is essential for health and wellbeing. It keeps your chi flowing right. Combining exercise with nature, eg swimming and hiking, can be especially uplifting. It connects you to the sacred, because everything comes from and is divinity, including nature.

Can't get out? Google home exercise plans. Even if you're bedridden, there are exercises you can do lying down. As for diet, everything in moderation including moderation. Skip fads; they're cash cows. The best thing you can do for your health is not stress about it. Fear depresses your immunity and other systems and bums out your vibe. Trust the divine to lead you to the path that's right for you.

Nurture your mental health during isolation by staying connected. Join self-help groups on social media and video chat with people who'll elevate you. Google how to get the emotional tools to deal with challenges. Use whatever services you need to feel sane, and don't hesitate to call helplines. This is a chance to straighten your head.

Anxiety and depression can become a self-feeding cycle, a comfy pair of slipper socks. Stay in inertia and you miss your life. God put you here for a purpose, and it's not to hide under the covers. What better time to figure out how to make your life count? Without jobs we in many cases loathe sucking all our energy and brain power, we have blessed time to find out what we actually want.

Prime time to break addictions, too. Many of us are stuck in a downward spiral until we see the light and start shifting from self-destruction to self-care and in time, self-love. In the sim it can be easy to get disenchanted and give up. You have a right to feel that way. The sim is all kinds of screwed up. It's full of suffering, and it's okay to feel angry about that.

It helps to understand that it's all for a reason. The sim is designed as a Matrixy, Inceptiony reality, because we as divinity made it that way. Yeah, think about that—if you come from the source and you are the source, it means *you* created life. *Woah* on that a bit.

When we were God—one infinite light—and we first observed ourself and realized how awesome we were, we wanted more. More godness, more awesome. We knew our own radness, but we couldn't experience that radness, because there was nothing *but* radness. No yardstick. To truly experience our radness, we had to create a reality that seemed to be the opposite of what we were: limited, separate, dense. We hid our god selves in meat suits so that, through trials that opened up our consciousness bit by bit, we could find our godness again.

Trials wake you up to your godly self. You then realize you are not limited, or separate, or dense. Illusion, all.

Then you get to roll around in the glory of your god nature and experience it in a whole new way, in form rather than as boundless light. You get to enjoy being a god in the flesh, until you ascend to higher realms and enjoy being a god in whatever form you choose— sometimes physical, sometimes astral, sometimes divine light, and infinite other potentials. This is the point of life. This is what we came for. That's why we hang on through the omni shambles, to get to the rad.

Hold on to that. Know that however bad things are, you're jetpacking to the light. Any moment you could have a breakthrough that'll catapult you into that extraordinary moment of enlightenment when divine love blasts out all the pain.

Courage. You are not life's victim. You do have the power to get what you want. Don't let your demons win. It's time to quit giving them your power.

Self-mastery becomes difficult when you keep handing control over to drugs, alcohol and medications that wreck your mind and body and muzzle your spirit. Consider natural and holistic alternatives (such as meditation) for less extreme cases where possible, along with healing practices like qigong, tummo and Kriya Yoga, which can all accelerate enlightenment.

Angelic healing is also yours for the taking. Call on the Angel of Healing—one of many powerful female angels—and Archangel Raphael. Heal yourself with a healing mantra. Repeat it in your mind or out loud during medo, in the shower, loading the dishwasher. "I

command you God/ Goddess/Milo to heal my body now."
Hand your issue over to the divine and follow the signs
to a solution that won't fry your brain.

Just don't grasp. Desperation kicks your sacred
connection. It's fear, not faith. Trust that every
experience is a teacher and whatever you need, God's got
you if you only believe. Stop fighting and striving and
just *let* the divine manifest in your life. Physical healing
often begins with emotional healing, so be prepared for
divinity to start there. Don't cringe away from going
within. Gazing into the dark mirror is the only way to see
the light.

A WARM FUZZY FACEPLANT

How does it feel? Enlightenment is like faceplanting in a
meadow of pegasus wings. It's the ultimate … till you hit
greater ultimates.

That starburst of unicornism will be unlike anything
you've experienced. Transcendental medos, astral travel,
split consciousness—a smorgasbord of weird might've
come before. But once you reach enlightenment, you'll
know the difference.

In that moment of satori, the sim falls away. It's
different for everyone, but most share the sensation of
momentarily becoming pure consciousness. That
awareness is omniscient, unlimited, and able to move at
light speed. This sudden liberation comes with
overpowering feelings of pure love, joy and peace. You

become your god nature.

Some touch and tour infinity on a cosmic joyride. Others are simply wrapped in the bliss of infinite oneness. However it happens for you, you'll know it's distinct from previous journeys because you'll come back feeling reborn.

Golden feelings may linger on your return from rapture. Joy and unconditional love stay with you. Serenity fills you come what may, because you have a euphoric understanding that nothing matters and everything's perfect. You fear nothing because you know the sim is just an illusion. Omniscience and oneness may stick around somewhat, giving you the ability to sense how things will turn out. You may see light in everything around you and feel so weightless that you seem to float rather than walk. These are all aspects of god realization, your god nature shining through.

If your satori lasts a long time, all that marinating in divine energy might make you feel physically unstable when you get back. Enlightenment is a ginormic vibe hike, and you may feel a tad like a nuclear reactor. Hone in on the energy. However you see it in your third eye (mind's eye), use strong intent to picture it pouring back into your body. It may appear as violet light streaming from your palms. Redirect it back inside through portals in the back of your wrists, or do what your guide tells you to do. Then bask in your unicorny glory.

Don't wanna DIY? Some people have scored immediate enlightenment through a master's blessing via online satori transmissions, and by darshan, the sight of a saint. However you become enlightened, use the *I, Unicorn* toolkit to carry you through your odyssey.

SATORRIFIC...ISH

...Hoo-kay, so, there's this thing called impermanence. As in, don't attach too hard to anything, because nothing lasts. Including enlightenment.

What! *That* wasn't in the brochure. Enlightenment is touted as the dot-com, a happy ever after deal. But in many ways it's just the beginning.

It's not that it fades at once. In fact, it might be the first of a few satoris. In my case, I wasn't quite on board with the idea of God. Even though when white light came out of the dark and exploded through me and then exploded *me* (astrally of course), I didn't recognize it for what it was: the big G. To really get my attention, God had to come back a few months later once I was ready and do a specific *ta-da!*

God revealed itself as a cluster of stars that then trickled into me, merging us. (The big G of course is neither male nor female. Light also isn't its only form. Being everything that is, it can use any interface—human, burning bush, spatula.) This was an even more epic experience than enlightenment, even though it wasn't a magical mystery ride like my satori. It was quiet, restful, but earthshaking to be one with God. That bond lasted a long time.

In hindsight, I'd experienced the big G many times. We hung out as a shared consciousness often in early childhood. This happens with many kids, as they're still in God's hands, till their programming solidifies and they start buying into the sim and tuning out the truth. Later, it was a touch of God's peace that I experienced in the stillness of meditation. Then I met the endless white light for the first time in a near death experience. At that phase I was still refusing to engage with the idea of God, so I didn't recognize it for what it was.

For you, enlightenment and becoming one with God may be separate experiences too, even though in essence they're the same. Enlightenment is meeting your divine self, while meeting God is meeting the source. Or they could happen together. Or they could split into various satoris. God likes to keep us on our toes, and no two people have the same experience.

But yep, over time, enlightenment fades. It's all part of the plan. Consider enlightenment that first lesson of senior year, where the teacher outlines the theory you'll be learning. She spells it out, gives you supporting hypotheses and equations and data, then says, "Now *you* do it." Pracs, tests, revision, exams—then presto, here's your grade.

Satori shows you who you truly are, what you're capable of, what the point is. It fills you with divine knowledge and love and bliss. Then God drops the mic and trundles off, leaving you to work out the rest. This isn't as harsh as it sounds. If you truly want to become a god, you need to learn to stand alone with no one holding your hand. You have to realize your own power.

Once you're enlightened, your ego will climb that and declare that it makes you uBeR sPeCiaL and turn you into an UbEr wAnG. The sim'll get you back in its claws with fear and doubt. You'll derp out and regress to materialism and narcissism and all the things that only keep you locked here. Your divine and astral connections could teeter, even vamoose. Hard knocks will attempt to break down your delusion. When you realize you've fallen from grace, you could feel like you've failed.

This is not failure. This is the plan. Once you float down from Cloud Nine, you're *meant* to flap and flounder as you puzzle out how the hell to apply that sacred wisdom in the sim. It's no rainbow ride to face everything you thought you knew and burn it down. Enlightenment is a spiritual enema. The shitstorms that follow are the crap coming out, and it's a shitnado of unicorn crap. Unicornism ain't for fainters, folks. But however wild the storm gets, it's still better than being blind, the way you were before you became a unicorn.

In time you remember what your satori taught you: how nothing matters, everything's perfect, there's nothing to fear. You apply this to your life in a practical way. You make an effort to humble yourself and surrender once more. Compassion, honesty and mindfulness return. You realize you're stronger and wiser and radder than you were pre-satori. And when divine peace trickles back, it's even more special than your satori, because this time God's not doing it through you. You're doing it *yourself*. This is how you become a god.

And lo, once you start counting on your own strength and wisdom instead of using divinity as a crutch, suddenly, God. The reunion might not be as explosive or phenomenal as first contact, but it can be even better. More realistic and comfy—the marriage after the honeymoon.

God may speak to you sometimes in the lead up to its return. Its presence will become clearer before it fills you again—perhaps not as richly as before, but that's because you're in this together now. That's my experience, anyway.

This is where I'm at, so I can't tell you personally where the road goes from there. God assures me that with faith, anything is possible. Stories abound of enlightened ones who've persisted in pure surrender, refusing to let the sim fool them for long, until they've reached the highest levels of mastery. Cue healing powers, miracles, resurrection, ascension.

So never give up. God's always leading you; all you have to do is follow. Just use your checklist:

be ~ breathe ~ unite ~ detach ~
be mindful ~ meditate ~ elevate

YOUR UNICORNY TOOLKIT

GET IT DONE, SON

Now you know the drill. All you have to do to become enlightened is be, and self-mastery is a way to do that. These three easy-squeezy medo techniques will help you get there. If medo is an absolute impossibility for you, don't fret, pet. Just wanting enlightenment, being open to it, and using mindfulness can get you far. For those who can medo, these practices will turbocharge you on the path to unicornism.

First up is a basic medo method. Medo will elevate you organically, but to put yourself in the fast lane, mash it up with the elevation exercise. Better still, mush both with the realization technique. For super efficiency, make it a burger with the lot and toss in *Om namo narayani* at the start.

Medo with devotion and without expectation, knowing that God will always bring you exactly what you need, when you need it, how you need it. Don't grasp;

remember, desperation is fear, and fear blocks God. Just be, trust, and surrender—unite. Just be unicorn.

I send everyone who reads this a blessing: May you get totally and blissfully unicorned.

MEDITATION

Medo every morning if possible to access the sacred peace that will bring you enlightenment.

1. Sit or lie with your spine comfortably straight, eyes either closed or focused slightly down.
2. White light yourself, take three deep breaths each held to a count of three, and let all your muscles melt.
3. Bring your mind back whenever it wanders by focusing on your breath, reciting a mantra like *Om namo narayani*, or picturing your happy place.

ELEVATION

Put your vibe in hyperdrive with this technique from the storm spirit (I swear that's not as Crazytown as it sounds. Medo and shoot the breeze with it next time there's a storm. It's very awesome). This will elevate your consciousness toward enlightenment; it did for me.

1. Picture your body as empty, like blown glass. Then see it as many small flames. Use strong intent to make them vibrate.
2. Imagine the flames turning white. Make them vibrate.
3. See them turning clear. Make them vibrate, then hold.

REALIZATION

The Who Am I self-inquiry technique by Indian sage Ramana Maharshi has helped many get enlightened. Use it as many times as you need to reach and return to the desired state.

1. Ask yourself, who am I? Inside your body, laser in on that sense of self-awareness - the specific feeling of "I". You might sense it in your heart, mind or core. But that sensation can't be you, because you're the one who's aware of that sensation. So you need to keep digging.

2. Zoom in on that feeling and ask again, who am I? This may produce a new sensation, thought or emotion. Zoom in on *that*. And realize again, you're the one *experiencing* that thought or feeling. It still isn't you.

3. Who am I? *Who am I?* Keep asking and zooming, again and again. Eventually, everything will go still, and you'll touch on an expansive peace that feels different to the "I". *That* is who you truly are.

UNICORNISM: GET IN THE SADDLE

UNICORNY TALES

I, Unicorn is all about you. Want to tell your story? If the apocalypse has seen you change your life, find your purpose, start a cause, get enlightened, or do something else rad, your story could star in a future book. Share it in a YouTube video (preferably in unicorn costume) – drop the link in the comments on my Unicorny Tales vid – and/or post it on social media (follow and tag me) and in the I, Unicorn Facebook Group. #iunicorn #unicornytales

YOU GOT UNICORNED COMPETITION

Turn yourself into a unicorn with a SnapChat unicorn filter, or snap or film yourself, a friend or a pet being a unicorn. Make a horn, ponytail your hair at the front like a horn, or don a unicorn suit and prance around like a unicorn should. You can turn it into a prank and surprise someone, saying, "You got unicorned!" Rather stay off camera? Surprise someone or a pet with a unicorn toy or your shih tzu-turned-unicorn (tin foil makes for an easy unihorn). Pin an ice cream cone unihorn to someone's forehead if they won't get too peeved. Invent your own way of unicorning. Do anything so long as it's a bit unicorn. Post your unicorny self on social media or in the I, Unicorn Facebook Group and tag me (#iunicorn #yougotunicorned). Or upload your video/vid link to Instagram and tag me @iunicornbook, the Facebook group, or the Calling All Unicorns You Got Unicorned Competition video on YouTube. Tag me and use the hashtags. **Competition ends 31 JULY 2020.** Winner gets a unicorn, or probably a $50 Amazon gift card.

WHATCHA WANT?

Did you find *I, Unicorn* useful? Tell me how on social media or in the Facebook I, Unicorn Group. I'm planning more books on how to make your life radder, so tell me what you want them to be about. What have you always wanted to know? How to meet God? Manifest anything you want? Make souffles that never fall? Let me know on social media or post in I, Unicorn.

THE UNICAUSE

Want to be more unicorn? Tell others about *I, Unicorn*. How often do you read a book or blog with tips you're totally going to use to improve your life … then forget all about it? Talking and writing about something glues the data to your brain so you can actually put it to use.

Also, if you review this book, the site will promote it to more people who need peace right now. Even a sentence will do. Thanks for doing your bit for the cause!

ACKNOWLEDGEMENTS

Thank you Daniel Mitel for a fabulous foreword. It's an honor to have the support of an accomplished master whose book *Journeys into the Heart* changed my life.

Cosmic gratitude to my publisher Mary Gudzenovs (Maz the Marvelous). Your patience is as limitless as the omniverse – and thanks for the bazillionth time for saving my life with your mad psychic skills. A shout out to Vanessa Forsyth for all your help, and for wrapping my brain around publishing in such a narrow window (with giggles).

Big feels to my beta readers, the wonderful Diane Hester and the Goddess of Awesome Michelle Bawden, and my rock star of a promoter Shelly Wilson. Bless you sensational authors Carolyn Haines and Terrie Leigh Relf for your support, advice and general brilliance over the years.

Warm fuzzies to my gorgeous friends and family, especially my very special mother Elizabeth for her spiritual grounding, wisdom and support. Epic air hugs to my uber-amazing teachers in the upper, earthly and sideways spheres, including my satori captain Jimmy.

Finally, infinite luvs to the big G, and to King M, my personal big G.

Anyone I've forgotten, know that I heart you!

www.ingramcontent.com/pod-product-compliance
Lightning Source LLC
Chambersburg PA
CBHW072157020426
42334CB00018B/2050